# HUSBANDS SUPPLIED

A Farce in One Act

by

FALKLAND L. CARY

SAMUEL FRENCH

LONDON
NEW YORK  TORONTO  SYDNEY  HOLLYWOOD

Copyright © 1939 by Falkland L. Cary
All Rights Reserved

*HUSBANDS SUPPLIED* is fully protected under the copyright laws of the British Commonwealth, including Canada, the United States of America, and all other countries of the Copyright Union. All rights, including professional and amateur stage productions, recitation, lecturing, public reading, motion picture, radio broadcasting, television and the rights of translation into foreign languages are strictly reserved.

ISBN 978-0-573-02109-1

www.samuelfrench.co.uk
www.samuelfrench.com

---

For Amateur Production Enquiries

United Kingdom and World
excluding north america
plays@samuelfrench.co.uk
020 7255 4302/01

Each title is subject to availability from Samuel French, depending upon country of performance.

---

CAUTION: Professional and amateur producers are hereby warned that HUSBANDS SUPPLIED is subject to a licensing fee. Publication of this play does not imply availability for performance. Both amateurs and professionals considering a production are strongly advised to apply to the appropriate agent before starting rehearsals, advertising, or booking a theatre. A licensing fee must be paid whether the title is presented for charity or gain and whether or not admission is charged.

The Professional Rights in this play are controlled by Samuel French (Concord Theatricals), Aldwych House, London WC2B 4HN.

No one shall make any changes in this title for the purpose of production. No part of this book may be reproduced, stored in a retrieval system, or transmitted in any form, by any means, now known or yet to be invented, including mechanical, electronic, photocopying, recording, videotaping, or otherwise, without the prior written permission of the publisher. No one shall upload this title, or part of this title, to any social media websites.

The right of Falkland L. Cary to be identified as author of this work has been asserted in accordance with Section 77 of the Copyright, Designs and Patents Act 1988.

TO
GWEN WILKINSON CRUNCH

## CHARACTERS

(In the order of their appearance.)

MRS. MAY (proprietress of the " Husbands Supplied " Bureau).
MISS JONES (her assistant).
MRS. WUFF
MRS. BEE
MISS WAFF } (Demand).
MISS CRUNCH
AN OLD LADY
THE MAN (Supply).

SCENE.—The office of the " Husbands Supplied " Matrimonial Bureau.

# HUSBANDS SUPPLIED

SCENE.—*The office of the " Husbands Supplied " Matrimonial Bureau. The office is precisely similar to the Domestic Registry office in the old days when maids could be obtained therefrom.*

*Some sort of a small desk or counter in the background, on which are laid ledgers, pens and ink.*

*Chairs line the walls; notices are displayed on the walls. A cheap print of " When did you last see your father? " hangs, appropriately enough, on the wall.*

*Two doors—one* L. *leads to the hall—one* R. *to an inner office and mystery.*

MRS. MAY *rings a small bell and* MISS JONES *enters from the inner office.* MRS. MAY *is a voluminous figure with a toupé, an adequate figure and a Presence.* MISS JONES *has none of the three.*

MRS. MAY. Everything ready, Miss Jones? There'll be a lot of them answering the door to-day.

MISS JONES. Indeed, madam?

MRS. MAY. Yes! It's Wednesday. We always get a lot of applications for husbands the first half of the week. The husbands have run away from the cold remainder of Sunday's roast.

MISS JONES. Don't husbands like cold meat, madam?

MRS. MAY. No man likes anything cold, Miss Jones. They may tell you they do, but don't believe them. All men are sheiks. The quieter they look, the bigger dirty dogs they are. I have had men in this office who looked as though butter wouldn't melt in their mouths, and, believe me or believe me not, they'd ruin the moral character of an iceberg.

Miss Jones. They're not all like that, are they?

Mrs. May. Yes, they are. They cling together like a pack of wolves. If you ever hear one man say of another that he's a decent fellow, you may take my word for it that he's the most indecent thing you've ever come across in your life.

Miss Jones. You've been married yourself, madam?

Mrs. May. Certainly. Three times.

Miss Jones. Did they all die, madam?

Mrs. May. They all passed away.

Miss Jones. It must be wonderful to be married three times. Do tell me about your husbands.

Mrs. May. There's nothing much to tell. My first was an actor. He used to tour the provinces, and came home for week-ends—occasionally. I called him "Faith." My second was a little rabbit of a man with asthma and a chest protector. I called him "Hope."

Miss Jones. And the third?

Mrs. May. Oh! the third was a lonely bachelor, who couldn't get his socks mended, and so I called him "Charity."

Miss Jones. And they all went west?

Mrs. May. Yes! "Faith" got killed in a motor accident when he was driving the car with his right hand, and making love to someone else's wife with his left.

Miss Jones. That must be very difficult to do.

Mrs. May. Not at all. "Faith" was left-handed. "Hope" got scalded to death when his hot-water bottle burst.

Miss Jones. Oh, madam, how tragic!

Mrs. May. Tragic—I should think so indeed—a brand-new hot-water bottle.

Miss Jones. And "Charity"?

Mrs. May. "Charity," I regret to say, had the stupidity and inconsideration to swallow a whole packet of weed killer, after I had spent a good hour trying to persuade him to come to a bargain sale with me.

## HUSBANDS SUPPLIED.

Miss Jones. My goodness! What was he doing with the weed killer?

Mrs. May (*darkly*). I often wondered. We hadn't a garden.

Miss Jones. I don't quite understand how you run the Bureau, madam.

Mrs. May. It's quite simple. When you want a maid, or when you lose a maid, what do you do? Go to the Bureau and get another. Well, it's the same thing here. If you want a husband or lose a husband, come along here, put your name down, and state your requirements. Fee, one guinea per husband, and no responsibility taken for subsequent proceedings—legal or otherwise.

Miss Jones. My! And do you get a lot of ladies here looking for husbands?

Mrs. May. Thousands of them. Big ones—little ones—fat ones—thin ones—young ones—old ones—pretty ones—and ones as ugly as the devil. There's always a shortage of good maids, and there's always a shortage of husbands good or bad. Now, don't forget your duty is to write down particulars of clients and the sort of husbands they want in that big ledger.

(*There's a loud knocking at the door.*)

Ah! an early bird after a worm. Show her in.

(*Enter* Mrs. Wuff—*furs, accent, scent, more furs, and more accent.*)

Good morning, madam.

Mrs. Wuff. Good morning.

Mrs. May. What can I do for you?

Mrs. Wuff. Well, what I really want is a husband.

Mrs. May. I can see that. Will you kindly give my assistant the full particulars. Name, age (approximately, of course), description, nature, requirements.

Mrs. Wuff. Lucretia Wuff—Mrs. Wuff—I am a widow.

Mrs. May. Oh! Divorced, bigamist or grass?

Mrs. Wuff. Well, certainly not grass.

Mrs. May. Not grass—hard court, eh? Put that down, Miss Jones. Your age?

Mrs. Wuff. Well, thirty—five.

Mrs. May. Thirty-five, Miss Jones. Plus fifteen.

Mrs. Wuff. What do you mean by plus fifteen? I am not fifty.

Mrs. May. Oh, no, madam. That's not your age, that's your handicap. What sort of husband do you wish for?

Mrs. Wuff. Oh, something exciting.

Mrs. May. Something exciting—ahem! Put her down as an optimist, Miss Jones. And his age?

Mrs. Wuff. Oh, about twenty-three or twenty-four.

Mrs. May. Twenty-three or twenty-four. Put down baby snatcher after optimist. And now habits?

Mrs. Wuff (*turns up right*). Oh, I'm not particular. He must dance well, of course, and mix cocktails, and not want to go to bed too early, and be able to play jazz, and know something about racing, and be able to act and swim, and drive a car, and play a decent hand at bridge, and——

Mrs. May. Have you got all that down, Miss Jones?

Miss Jones. Yes, madam. He must be able to dance well, play a decent hand at jazz, and not want to mix cocktails in bed.

(*There's another knock at the door.*)

Mrs. Wuff. Do you think that is—a man?

Mrs. May. Judging from the boldness of the knock, I should say no! (*She opens the door and admits* Mrs. Bee.) What, you again, Mrs. Bee? I'm afraid I haven't anything to suit you.

(Mrs. Bee *is slight and young, wearing dark spectacles, a muffler and long coat.*)

Mrs. Bee (*in a timid voice*). I know, but may I come in and wait, please? Someone might turn up.

Mrs. May. Certainly, Mrs. Bee. Come in.

(Mrs. Bee *walks across to the chair*—R.)

Mrs. Bee. Thank you.

Mrs. Wuff (*turning round*). I presume, Mrs. May, that I have an option on whatever man arrives first?

Mrs. May. I couldn't guarantee anything of that sort. Will you sit down, madam?

Mrs. Wuff. Thank you.

(*There's another knock at the door.*)

Mrs. Bee }
Mrs. Wuff } (*together*). Ah!

(Mrs. May *is now behind the desk.* Miss Jones *goes towards the door, at which all are looking. Enter* Miss Waff. *She is a tall and gaunt young woman, whose outlook on the world is not biased by an undue proportion of good looks.*)

Mrs. May. Good morning.

Miss Waff (*heavily*). Good morning. I have been advised to take a husband.

Mrs. May. Advised! By whom? Your doctor?

Miss Waff. No, by my clergyman.

Mrs. May. The wicked old gentleman.

Mrs. Wuff. Disgusting!

Mrs. May. And what sort of a husband do you require, madam?

Miss Waff. I don't mind. Only one thing is important. He must be a man with a soul.

Mrs. May. A what?

Miss Waff. A soul.

Mrs. May. What sort of a soul?

Miss Waff (*again heavily*). A soul that craves for the wide open spaces, the rustling of trees in the moonlight, and the perfume of roses in early June. Have you any husbands free at the moment?

Mrs. May. Not any souley ones.

Miss Waff. Perhaps I had better call again. (*She moves towards the door.*)

Mrs. May. Your best chance, madam, would be to sit and wait; something with a soul might blow in. I had one last week—but he was snapped up in no time by a lady who kept a lodging-house in Brighton. My assistant will take all particulars—Miss Jones.

(MISS WAFF *moves over to the desk.*)

MRS. MAY. Now, Mrs. Bee, you've been coming every day for the last month. What sort of a husband do you really want? A soul or a thriller?

MRS. BEE (*hesitatingly*). Oh—just any sort of a husband—I'll tell you if one comes in who would suit me.

MRS. WUFF. I should warn you, madam, that I have a prior claim to you on any man this morning.

MISS JONES. That's all, thank you.

MRS. MAY. Will you sit down, Miss Waff?

(MISS WAFF *takes a seat on the other side of* MRS. WUFF.)

MRS. WUFF (*aggressively*). You get all sorts here, don't you?

MRS. MAY. It takes all sorts to make a marriage.

(*Another knock. All the ladies stiffen at once. The knock is repeated.*)

ALL. Ah——

MRS. MAY. Come in.

(*A tall, gaunt and rugged spinster enters; she is dressed in black and rust—an evil and sombre toque almost, but alas! not entirely, eclipses her countenance. She takes a severe and assured glance round the room, sniffs, and then walks to the counter.*)

MISS JONES. Yes—madam?

MISS CRUNCH. Are you the proprietress—I said, "Are you the proprietress?"

MISS JONES. Oh, no, ma'am——

MRS. MAY. I am Mrs. May. What can I do for you?

MISS CRUNCH. I have called for a husband.

MRS. MAY. Oh, yes! Your own or someone else's?

MISS CRUNCH. I am not married.

MRS. MAY. And what is your name?

MISS CRUNCH. Crunch.

MRS. MAY. I beg your pardon?

## HUSBANDS SUPPLIED.

Miss Crunch. I said Crunch.
Mrs. May. Miss Jones, take down Miss Crunch's particulars.
Miss Jones. Name, please?
Miss Crunch. Crunch—Sarah Crunch.
Miss Jones. Scarah Scrunch—thank you. Age?
Miss Crunch. Forty-one.

(*An audible titter from the listening ladies.*)

Miss Jones. Spinster?
Miss Crunch. Certainly.
Miss Jones. Nature?
Mrs. May. The answer is a lemon, Miss Jones.
Miss Jones. Thank you. Lemon spinster. What sort of a husband do you require, madam?
Miss Crunch. A worker. I said, "A worker." Have you any husbands in now?
Mrs. May. No, madam, but one may turn up any moment now. Will you take a seat?

(Miss Crunch *sits beside* Miss Waff.)

Miss Waff. I find this waiting extremely unpleasant.
Mrs. Wuff. Waiting for a husband is always unpleasant.
Miss Crunch. Stuff and nonsense.
Mrs. Wuff. I beg your pardon. (*With great dignity.*)
Miss Crunch. I said, "Stuff and nonsense."
Mrs. Wuff. And was that observation addressed to me——?

(*Again there is a knock on the door. This is listened to in dead silence, and then it is repeated.*)

All. Ah——

(*The door is opened, and a little* Old Lady *comes in, rosy-cheeked and dressed in a manner suggestive of the country.*)

Old Lady (*peeping in*). I understand one can hire a husband here.

Mrs. Wuff. Well, my goodness! ⎫
Miss Crunch. Upon my word! ⎪
Mrs. Bee. Oh, dear me! ⎬ (*Together.*
Miss Waff. Revolting! ⎪ *Noise.*)
Miss Jones. Well, I never! ⎭
Mrs. May. Not *hire*, madam—not *hire*, please.
Old Lady. I am very sorry. Perhaps there has been some mistake. I was told——
Mrs. Wuff. You don't *hire* husbands.
Old Lady. I beg your pardon—perhaps I should have said I wanted to *buy* a husband.
Mrs. May. You can *engage* a husband if you wish.
Old Lady. Ah! "Engage"—that's the word I should have used. Well, may I have one?
Mrs. May. One what?
Old Lady. One husband.
Mrs. May. All these ladies are waiting for a husband—perhaps you will wait with them?
Old Lady. Oh, dear! Will I have to wait? Don't you keep them in stock?
Mrs. May. In stock!
Old Lady. Dear! dear! dear! dear! Have I said something wrong again?
Mrs. May. This is not a grocer's shop, madam.
Old Lady. No, indeed, I'm sure it isn't.
Mrs. May. Will you give my assistant the particulars, please.
Old Lady. Well, you see, I just want a husband.
Mrs. May (*with heavy sarcasm*). Any particular shape or size?
Old Lady. No, I don't think so—I think I'd like a big one.
Miss Waff. A big one!
Old Lady. With blue eyes.
Miss Crunch. With blue eyes!
Old Lady. I beg your pardon?
Miss Crunch. I said, "With blue eyes."
Old Lady. So you want one with blue eyes, too. They're so honest, aren't they, dear?
Mrs. Wuff. This is getting beyond a joke—I'm not

going to waste my time here any longer. (*To the* OLD
LADY.) Are you really telling us that you have come
here to look for a husband?

MRS. WUFF. That's a different thing altogether.

OLD LADY. But why? I don't understand.

MRS. WUFF. At your age—you shouldn't want a
husband. At my age it's quite different.

MISS CRUNCH. That's a good one.

MRS. WUFF (*to* MISS CRUNCH). How dare you!

MISS CRUNCH. I said, "That's a good one."

MISS WAFF. I haven't been asked for my opinion——

MRS. WUFF. No, you haven't, and you needn't give it.

MISS WAFF. But if I were, I would say that this lady
has as good a right to a husband as anyone else.

MRS. BEE (*unexpectedly*). Hear, hear.

MRS. WUFF. Indeed! And who asked you to speak?

MRS. MAY. For that matter, who asked you?

MISS CRUNCH. Perhaps he got tired of you—that's a
good one.

MRS. WUFF. Please mind your own business.

MISS CRUNCH. I said, "That's a good one."

MRS. MAY (*to the* OLD LADY). Won't you sit down,
madam?

OLD LADY. Thank you. (*To* MRS. WUFF.) I'll sit
by you, dear, if I may.

MRS. WUFF. I suppose I can't stop you—but I think
all this is perfectly ridiculous.

(*Another knock at the door.*)

ALL. Ah!

OLD LADY. Now I wonder if that might be a man.

(*The knock is repeated.*)

MRS. MAY. Come in.

(*The door is opened and a hand is put round the door
and a newspaper flung on the floor.*)

BOY'S VOICE. Your paper, mum.

(MISS JONES *sadly picks up the paper and looks at it.*)

Miss Jones. "Daily Mail."
Miss Crunch (*delivering herself of a stupendous joke*). "Daily Mail"! Why, that's what we're waiting for.

(*This is received in stony silence.*)

Miss Crunch (*in paroxysms*). I said, "That's what we're all waiting for."
Miss Waff. If that is meant as a joke, I consider it extremely vulgar.
Mrs. Wuff. Disgusting.
Old Lady (*suddenly*). Of course, "Daily Male"—I see it now. (*Laughing.*)
Miss Crunch. I said, "That's what we're all waiting for."
Mrs. May. And very good, too.

(*They all laugh except* Mrs. Wuff *and* Miss Waff.)

Mrs. Wuff. As I said before, this is all perfectly ridiculous. I have come here to find a husband, and I find a room of sniggering women.
Miss Waff. I beg your pardon, I wasn't sniggering. How dare you say such a thing.
Miss Crunch. She'd dare anything.
Mrs. May. Now, then, ladies, ladies, please.
Miss Crunch. I said——

(*But again there is a knocking at the door, and all the ladies stiffen.*)

All. Ah!——
Miss Waff. Is that one?
Mrs. May (*holding up her head for silence*). Ssh!

(*The knocking—very timid, deprecatory knocking—is repeated.*)

That's one. Come in.

(*The door opens slowly, and* The Man *comes in. He is—whatever you like, and of the same age, and dressed in the same way. Obviously he is in a new and rather strange situation, but he is going to make the best of it.*)

Mrs. May. Miss Jones, please shut the door behind the gentleman. (*In a whisper.*) And lock it.

(The Man *half turns round as this manœuvre is completed, and then moves a few steps into the room.*)

The Man. Excuse me—but are any of you ladies looking for a husband?

(*The ladies rise as one lady.*)

All. Yes.

(The Man *rapidly surveys them, and then hurriedly turns to the door.*)

The Man. Oh!—— I think I'll call another day.

Miss Crunch. Stop.

The Man. I beg your pardon?

Miss Crunch. I said, "Stop."

The Man (*hastening away*). No! I don't think I will, thank you.

Mrs. May. Are you looking for a wife?

The Man. I was—but it doesn't matter now. (*He tries the door.*) What's the matter with this door? Why, it's locked. (*He looks round in angry surprise, and his eye lights on* Miss Jones.) You locked it. I saw you.

Miss Jones. Ooo-er, what a frightful story.

The Man. You know you did. I can see the key in your hand.

Miss Jones. I wouldn't give up that key, not if you were to throttle me to death.

The Man. But I haven't the faintest wish to throttle you to death. But will you kindly open that door?

Mrs. May. If we do open the door, will you go away?

The Man. Certainly.

Mrs. May. Then we won't open it.

Mrs. Wuff. You came here to get a wife, and you'll have to have one. Personally, I should advise you take the one you like the look of best.

The Man. This sounds remarkably like intimidation.

Old Lady. Come in again, young man, you're quite safe.

THE MAN. I should feel far safer with the door open.
MRS. MAY. Won't you sit down, Mr. —— ?

(*She places a chair* c. *They all sit.*)

THE MAN. Smith.
MRS. MAY. Miss Jones, open that door. Now, Mr. Smith, I am the proprietress of "Husbands Supplied." I understand that you are in need of a situation.
THE MAN. Well, I certainly came here to look for a wife.
MRS. MAY. I can promise you we will have no difficulty in suiting you. Will you draw up your chairs, ladies?

(*A semi-circle is formed round* THE MAN. MRS. WUFF *attempts to get her chair in between that of* MISS CRUNCH *and* THE MAN. MISS CRUNCH *is having none of it.*)

MISS CRUNCH. No, you don't.
MRS. WUFF. Kindly make room for me.
MISS CRUNCH. I said, "No, you don't."
MRS. MAY. Now, ladies, please.

(MISS CRUNCH *slips her chair round left of* THE MAN.)

OLD LADY (*to* MISS WAFF). My dear, do you mind telling me what colour eyes he's got? I can't see from here.

(MISS WAFF *leaves the circle and gazes intently into* THE MAN'S *eyes.*)

Blue?
MISS WAFF. Deep Mediterranean blue.
MISS CRUNCH. Go away.
MISS WAFF. Are you addressing me?
MISS CRUNCH. Yes! I said, "Go away."
MISS WAFF (*returning to her seat*). What rudeness.
MRS. MAY. If any of you ladies would like to ask the applicant any questions——
MISS CRUNCH. Eat cheese?
THE MAN. I beg your pardon?
MISS CRUNCH. I said, "Eat cheese?"

## HUSBANDS SUPPLIED.

THE MAN (*a little taken aback*). Yes! I eat cheese.
MISS CRUNCH. Drink beer?
THE MAN. Yes, occasionally.
MISS CRUNCH. Pints or gallons?
THE MAN. Pints as a rule. (*Politely.*)
MRS. WUFF. Can you dance?
THE MAN. A little.
MRS. WUFF. Tango?
THE MAN. Indifferently.
MISS WAFF. Do you read?
THE MAN. Yes.
MISS WAFF. What?
THE MAN. "Daily Mail."
MISS CRUNCH. "Daily Mail"—that's a good one.
THE MAN. I don't quite understand.
MISS CRUNCH. I said, "That's a good one." Smoke tobacco?
THE MAN. Yes.
MISS CRUNCH. Clean about the house?
THE MAN. I hope so.
MRS. WUFF. And now about your references.
THE MAN. References?
MRS. WUFF. Yes! Previous employer.
MRS. MAY. The lady wants to know, have you been married before?
THE MAN. Yes.
MISS CRUNCH. Often?
THE MAN. No.
MISS WAFF. Is she alive?
MISS CRUNCH. Are *they* alive?
THE MAN. I don't know.
MRS. WUFF. Ah! a bigamist—this sounds interesting.
MISS WAFF. Are you a bigamist?
OLD LADY. What is a bigamist, my dears?
MRS. MAY. A man who makes two bites at a cherry.
OLD LADY. I don't at all understand what a bigamist is yet.
MISS CRUNCH. A damn fool.
MRS. MAY. Miss Crunch—Miss Crunch!

Miss Crunch. I said, "Damn fool." (*To* The Man.) Gambler?
The Man. No!
Miss Waff. You haven't answered the question yet. Are you a bigamist?
The Man. No!
Miss Waff. Then what happened to your first wife?
The Man. Separated.
Miss Waff. Divorced?
The Man. That sort of thing.
Old Lady. May I ask a few questions?
Mrs. May. Certainly.
Old Lady. Are you sober, honest and truthful?
The Man. Yes, I think so.
Miss Crunch. All three?
The Man. Yes!
Miss Crunch. Bosh!
Mrs. Wuff. You must understand that if I engage you, I shall expect you to take an interest in things I am interested in.
Miss Crunch. Men?
Mrs. Wuff. I beg your pardon?
Miss Crunch. I said, "Men?"
Mrs. Wuff (*to* The Man). Kindly stand up.

(The Man *does so.*)

Turn round.

(*He does so.*)

Miss Crunch. Teeth.

(*He shows his teeth.*)

Your own or somebody else's?
The Man. All my own.
Old Lady. Do you take cold easily, dear?
The Man. No!
Mrs. Wuff. Thank you. You may sit down.
Mrs. May. Any other questions, ladies?
Miss Crunch. No need for questions. I'll take him.
Miss Waff. You'll do nothing of the sort.

## HUSBANDS SUPPLIED.        21

Miss Crunch. I said, "I'll take him."
Miss Waff. As a matter of fact, I shall engage him.
Miss Crunch. I said——
Mrs. Wuff. There is no need to argue about it—I have already chosen him.
Miss Crunch (*standing up*). Come along.
The Man. But——
Mrs. Wuff (*seizing him, too*). Kindly let my husband go.
Miss Waff. Your husband—I have already engaged him.
The Man. But, ladies, really——
Old Lady. Now, my dears, you can't all take him—and just to save any argument I am going to have him myself.
Miss Crunch. Rubbish! ⎫
Mrs. Wuff. Ridiculous! ⎬ (*Together. Noise.*)
Miss Waff. Absurd! ⎭
Miss Crunch. Come along now—— ⎫
Mrs. Wuff. I tell you, I—— ⎬ (*Together.*
Miss Waff. I'm not going to—— ⎨ *Noise.*)
Old Lady. There's no use trying—— ⎭
Mrs. May. Ladies, be quiet, all of you—and sit down.

(*They all subside.*)

Please remember that this is my office. There need be no further argument—I have decided to engage him myself.
All. What?
Mrs. May. That is all, ladies—the bureau is closed for the day.
Miss Crunch. Robber—I said, "You're a robber."
Mrs. Wuff. You needn't think we're going to let you get away with him.
Mrs. May. Miss Jones, I expect you to stand by me.
Miss Jones (*fumbling in her bag*). Here you are. It's a guinea, isn't it?
Mrs. May. What's a guinea?
Miss Jones. The fee—I don't see why I shouldn't have him myself. I'm younger than any of you.

Miss Crunch. Liar!
The Man. May I be allowed to say a word?
Miss Crunch. I know—— You want me—come along.
Mrs. May. Let him go.
The Man. Ladies, may I be allowed to say a word? Since you can't all have me, why shouldn't I choose the one I like best?
Mrs. Wuff. Good gracious! Fancy a man choosing his wife!
The Man. I know it's not done nowadays, but I don't see any other way out of the difficulty.
Miss Crunch. Man's right. Sit down. (Miss Crunch *sits*.)
Mrs. May. Well, perhaps there's something in the idea. (Mrs. May *sits*.)
The Man. Are you all agreed?

(*They nod assent.*)

Good. Then won't you all sit down?

(*They sit down.*)

Good, again.

(*There is a pause.*)

Miss Crunch. Well!—— I'm still here. I said, "I'm still here."

(*There is no answer and the others signal to her to be silent.*)

Miss Waff. Will you be silent and allow him to make up his mind?
Mrs. Wuff (*smiling at him*). I don't think there will be any difficulty about that.
The Man. But you haven't told me yet what each of you has to offer me.
Mrs. May. Well, I never.
Miss Crunch. Man's right. I'll begin. I——
Miss Waff. I can——
Mrs. Wuff. With me——
Old Lady. If you—— } (*Together. Noise.*)
Miss Jones. I know——
Mrs. May. I offer——

THE MAN. Wouldn't it be better if you all spoke separately? Supposing you all spoke in order from the right.

MRS. MAY. Very well. Mrs. Bee.

MRS. BEE (*nervously*). Oh! I think I'll leave it to you, ladies.

MRS. MAY. Good. Mrs. Wuff.

MRS. WUFF. I can offer you all that the others can—and something else.

MISS CRUNCH. Hey! what's that—I said, "What's that?"

THE MAN. Don't interrupt, please.

MRS. WUFF (*intensely*). I can offer you—companionship.

MISS CRUNCH. That's a good one—I said, "That's a good one."

MRS. MAY. Time's up. Next, please.

MISS WAFF. I can offer you something infinitely bigger—something that transcends to oblivion and brings the joy of infinity. I can bring you——

MISS CRUNCH. Spit it out.

MRS. MAY. Silence, please.

MISS CRUNCH. I said—— (*But here* THE MAN *fortunately places his open hand across her mouth.*)

MISS WAFF. I can bring you—love.

MISS CRUNCH. Well, I never. That's a better one. I said, "That's a better one."

MRS. MAY. Will you be quiet, please? It's your turn now. What can you offer?

MISS CRUNCH (*without a moment's hesitation*). Beer and victuals.

THE MAN. Beer and what?

MISS CRUNCH. I said, "Beer and victuals."

MRS. MAY. Is that all?

MISS CRUNCH. Quite enough.

MRS. MAY. Very well, then. Miss Jones, since you insist on regarding yourself as a client——

MISS JONES. I can offer you—my heart.

MISS CRUNCH. Better have beer and victuals.

MRS. MAY. Is that all? Very well, I will speak last.

I can offer you a good home and house and a share in this office. Now then, choose.

OLD LADY. Just a moment—you seem to have forgotten me.

MRS. MAY. Oh, you're still playing, are you? Very well, then.

OLD LADY. I can offer you half—just exactly half a little farmhouse fifteen miles outside Maidstone in Kent. The river runs through the bottom of the meadow in front of the house, and the meadow is gay with orchids and bryony—white bryony and black—and willow throstle, and the sun sets at the back through the orchard and throws long black shadows on the ground—and if you like beer, why, remember we grow hops in Kent.

MRS. MAY. Is that all? Now—choose.

(THE MAN *thinks for a moment—then walks up and down a few steps in front of them.*)

THE MAN. Do you know, I find it impossible to make up my mind. You are all so attractive—and in so many ways. The beauty of Colette—charm of Mignonette—grace of Antoinette in you arrayed. Must I refuse you all because I admire you all?

MISS CRUNCH. I'm still here.

THE MAN. Yes! I know.

MISS CRUNCH. Well!

THE MAN. A moment, please. Let me think. Let me see—there are (*counting*) one, two, three, four, five, six, seven of you, and there are seven days of the week.

MISS CRUNCH. There's only five of them as well as me. She (*pointing to* MRS. BEE) isn't in it.

THE MAN. Six of you—why, that makes it even better. Supposing, now, you six were to share me.

ALL. Share you!

THE MAN. Yes! I should be husband of the first of you on the first day of the week—the second on the second, and so on. You see, in that way I should enjoy —Companionship on Mondays—Love on Tuesdays— Beer and—wasn't it victuals on Wednesdays? This lady's heart on Thursdays and the Bureau on Fridays—and that delightful meadow at Maidstone on Saturdays.

Miss Crunch. And what would you do on Sundays?

The Man. Sunday, my dear lady, is a day of rest.

Miss Waff. Well, I think that is the most abominable suggestion I have ever heard. He isn't a bigamist—he's a Mormon.

Mrs. May. Scandalous and disgraceful.

Mrs. Wuff. Intolerable. Haven't you eyes in your head, man?

Miss Jones (*regretfully*). I am afraid my people would never allow me.

Mrs. May. The whole thing's impossible.

All. Absolutely.

Mrs. May. Ladies, I propose that we adjourn to the other room and discuss this matter in private. Some arrangement will have to be made unless we all want to lose him.

Miss Crunch. You go away and discuss. I'll watch him.

Mrs. Wuff. I wouldn't trust that woman with any man.

Miss Waff. Certainly not.

Mrs. May. I know—Mrs. Bee, you are not interested in this gentleman?

Mrs. Bee. I—what. Oh, no, of course not. Why should I be?

Mrs. May. Very well—we will lock the outer door and give you the key, while we all arrange the affair in the other room. You stay here with him, and if he attempts to take the key from you—scream. (*Locking the door, and giving the key to* Mrs. Bee.)

Mrs. Bee. But I——

Mrs. May. Will that do, ladies?

Miss Waff. I think it is an excellent idea.

Mrs. Wuff. Certainly.

Mrs. May. Come along then.

(*She opens the door to the room, and the ladies file out—* Miss Jones *first, then the* Old Lady, *who blows a kiss to the man—then* MISS WAFF, *followed by* MRS. WUFF.)

MISS CRUNCH (*to* MRS. BEE). Now, then, no monkey tricks. I said, "No monkey tricks."

(*She goes out, followed by* MRS. MAY, *and the two are left alone.*)

THE MAN (*walking to the outer door*). God—what a mess. (*Trying the door.*) Locked all right.

(MRS. BEE *holds up the key.*)

I wonder is there anything I can do to persuade you to let me get out of this damned place. You see, it's all been a mistake.

MRS. BEE (*still in her pitched voice*). No mistake. You wanted a wife—you'll get a wife—several wives—six of them.

THE MAN. But you don't understand, I didn't come here to get a wife—I came to look for——

MRS. BEE. Someone else's wife, I expect.

THE MAN. Not someone else's—my own.

MRS. BEE. What!

THE MAN. Oh! it's a long sordid story—I can't possibly tell you all of it.

MRS. BEE. Tell me the spicy bits.

THE MAN. There—there aren't any spicy bits.

MRS. BEE. Sit down and tell me.

THE MAN. Will you let me out if I do?

MRS. BEE. I might. Sit down—now——

THE MAN. Well, you see, we were only married two years when I suppose I got worried over work, or careless, or something, and we——

MRS. BEE. Quarrelled.

THE MAN. Yes! About something silly, and from bad it got to worse, and then one day she left me.

MRS. BEE. Go on.

THE MAN. That's all.

MRS. BEE. That's very little. Didn't you try to get her to come back?

THE MAN. That's it. I couldn't. I didn't know where she had gone to.
MRS. BEE. Did you look for her?
THE MAN. Everywhere.
MRS. BEE. Hadn't she gone back to her mother and father?
THE MAN. She hadn't a mother or father.
MRS. BEE. Dear me—what a convenient sort of wife to have. But still I don't understand what you were doing in here looking for another wife?
THE MAN. I wasn't—I was looking for her. I thought she might be looking for another husband. Now, please, will you let me go?

(*From the back* MISS CRUNCH'S *voice is heard.*)

MISS CRUNCH. I'll have him, I say, I'll have him.

(*The voice is almost drowned in a shriek of protest from the others.*)

THE MAN. For mercy's sake, let me go before *that* comes back.
MRS. BEE. Certainly not. I had hoped that there might be something good in your story, but now it turns out that you are nothing more than a bad-tempered, selfish husband, and you deserve all you get.
THE MAN. But you promised——

(*Here the door is flung open and* MISS CRUNCH *enters, followed by the others.*)

MISS CRUNCH. That's all right. I'm to have you—I say I'm to have you.
MRS. MAY. Come back, you brazen hussy.
MRS. WUFF. Take her away from him.
MISS JONES (*entering*). Here, fair play—fair play.
MISS WAFF. I insist on my rights.
OLD LADY. I may be old, but I'm very tough, and I'll not give him up without a struggle.
THE MAN. Ladies—ladies. Please let me go.
MISS CRUNCH. All settled. (*To* MRS. BEE.) Give me the key.

ALL. Don't give it to her.
MRS. MAY. You can't have him. We're five to one. Now, sir, we have decided to accept your offer—we will share you.
THE MAN. My heavens! And whom do I begin with?
MISS CRUNCH. Me. Come along.
MRS. BEE (*unexpectedly*). Wait a moment.
MRS. MAY. And who asked you to speak?
MRS. BEE. Nobody—but he's coming home with me.
MISS CRUNCH. Dirty work. Dirty work. You shouldn't have left them together.
MRS. BEE. He's coming with me.
THE MAN. Well, I——
MRS. BEE. You're coming with me, aren't you—Charles?
THE MAN. Charles—how do you know my name?
MRS. BEE. Come over here—closer—closer—now.
THE MAN. I'm afraid I don't understand.
MRS. BEE (*taking off her glasses*). Look into my eyes—Charles.
MISS CRUNCH. Don't you do anything of the sort. I know the game. Sex appeal.
THE MAN. Phillipina—Good heavens—you! (*He seizes her in his arms.*)
MISS CRUNCH (*belabouring him with an umbrella*). Come off it—come off it!
MRS. MAY. You minx.
MISS WAFF. The basest treachery.
MRS. WUFF. You intriguing woman.
THE MAN. My Phillipina.
MISS CRUNCH. What's all this about Phillipina?
THE MAN. But you don't understand.
MRS. MAY. Understand what?
MRS. BEE (*who is taking off her coat and muffler and now stands revealed as a charming demoiselle of twenty-three*). This man—is my husband!
MISS CRUNCH. Oh, my garters.
THE MAN. Yes, it's quite true.
MRS. MAY. Then what were you doing here?

Mrs. Wuff. It's a put-up job between the two of them.

The Man. Ladies, I am sorry—really so very sorry to have deceived you all, but this is my wife. You see—we quarrelled—it was all my fault—and she left me. I looked for her everywhere, and then—it struck me as possible—I might find her here.

Mrs. May (*to* Mrs. Bee). And you?

Mrs. Bee. Well, you see. I'm afraid I wanted him to find me—and I couldn't go back myself, could I?—so I just thought he might happen to come here now—so that's all.

Mrs. Wuff. All—and I should think that's enough. Here have I spent a whole morning assisting two silly people to get married to each other again.

Mrs. Bee. We're awfully sorry.

Mrs. Wuff. I should think you are—I consider I have been shamefully deceived. (*Going to the door and speaking to* Mrs. May.) As for you, madam, I shall tell all my friends how I have been treated (*to the door, voice rises*) and I consider that your Bureau is nothing more than—a sanguinary swindle.

(*She goes out.*)

Miss Waff. I, too, have been deceived—and I shall go back and tell my clergyman—that he'll have to marry me himself.

Miss Crunch. That'll serve him right. Woman's a fool—well, game's up. I'm off.

The Man. But won't you let me——

Miss Crunch. I said, "Game's up." (*Going to the door.*) No fool like an old fool. I'll buy a pekinese instead. Good-bye.

Old Lady. Well, my dears, I hope you'll be very happy.

Mrs. Bee. That's just sweet of you. (*She kisses her.*)

Old Lady. Good-bye, little wife—don't do it again. (*To* The Man.) Good-bye, young man—be a little wiser next time.

The Man. Good-bye. (*Unexpectedly he kisses the* Old Lady.)

OLD LADY (*going to the door*). H'mm, I hoped you'd do that.

(*She goes out.*)

MRS. MAY. A pretty kettle of fish. Well, you both owe me a guinea.

THE MAN (*fumbling in his pockets*). Here you are.

MRS. MAY. Ten pounds—you must be very fond of her.

THE MAN. I am.

MRS. MAY. No fool like a young one. Thank you. Come along, Miss Jones.

(*She goes to the inner room.*)

MISS JONES (*to* MRS. BEE). Good-bye, ma'am.

MRS. BEE. Good-bye.

MISS JONES. Good-bye, sir.

THE MAN (*shaking her hand*). Good-bye.

MISS JONES (*hesitating*). Er—good-bye, sir.

THE MAN. Good-bye.

MISS JONES. Er—good-bye, sir.

MRS. BEE. Go on, Charles.

THE MAN. Go on, what——

MRS. BEE. Kiss her.

THE MAN. Oh! Lord, must I? (*He kisses her.*)

MRS. MAY (*at the door*). Miss Jones.

MISS JONES. Oh! coming, madam—coming.

(*She runs off.*)

MRS. BEE. And now——

THE MAN (*coming to her*). And now?

MRS. BEE. You'll never be brutal to me again?

THE MAN. Phillipina. Never—and you'll never run away from me again?

MRS. BEE. Never!

THE MAN (*about to kiss her*). Then, darling——

MRS. BEE. Darling——

(*But the door is opened and* MISS CRUNCH *appears.*)

Miss Crunch. Forgot to say. In cases of any trouble in the future, shall always be at home Wednesday nights.

Curtain.

Any character costumes or wigs needed in the performance of this play can be hired from Charles H. Fox Ltd, 184 High Holborn, London W C 1

www.ingramcontent.com/pod-product-compliance
Ingram Content Group UK Ltd.
Pitfield, Milton Keynes, MK11 3LW, UK
UKHW021849210426
5322IPUK00022B/549